PIANO • VOCAL • GUITAR

THE BEST OF LUTHER VANDROSS
THE BEST OF LOVE

S0-APQ-736

ISBN 0-7935-0291-8

HAL•LEONARD® CORPORATION

7777 W. BLUEMOUND RD. P.O. BOX 13819 MILWAUKEE, WI 53213

C O N T E N T S

100   ANY LOVE

94   GIVE ME THE REASON

12   THE GLOW OF LOVE

122   HERE AND NOW

44   A HOUSE IS NOT A HOME

107   I REALLY DIDN'T MEAN IT

56   IF ONLY FOR ONE NIGHT / CREEPIN'

26   IF THIS WORLD WERE MINE

21   NEVER TOO MUCH

40   PROMISE ME

6   SEARCHING

34   SINCE I LOST MY BABY

83   SO AMAZING

75   STOP TO LOVE

67   SUPERSTAR / UNTIL YOU COME BACK TO ME

88   THERE'S NOTHING BETTER THAN LOVE

49   'TIL MY BABY COMES HOME

114   TREAT YOU RIGHT

After an unprecedented six consecutive Platinum-plus albums, it seems only fitting that a special album of some of the best music by the premier black male vocalist of our time should finally be made available. Unlike other such packages, *THE BEST OF LUTHER VANDROSS, THE BEST OF LOVE* (Epic) contains not only this multitalented superstar's major chart hits but also delves into the master Vandross catalog to present more of the music that has made Luther the entertainer most cited as a major influence by up-and-coming vocalists.

As a writer, producer, and recording artist, Luther's innate ability to create sounds that touch the heart has been the key to his enduring success. His exciting live performances have made him an international entertainer of the highest caliber.

Nor has Luther simply channeled his talents into his own work. He's also produced records for boyhood idols Aretha Franklin, Dionne Warwick and Diana Ross. The list of Vandross triumphs also includes vocalist Cheryl Lynn and singer/actor Gregory Hines, whose Vandross-produced Epic debut spawned the 1988 hit "That Girl Wants To Dance With Me."

Luther's early musical instincts were strongly encouraged by his family, including piano lessons at the age of 3. An older sister sang with the doo-wop group The Crests (of "16 Candles" fame), and as Luther progressed through Taft High School, "it was Aretha Franklin, Diana Ross and Dionne Warwick who lit my fire," he recalls. After attending Western Michigan University, Luther returned to New York, where he held a variety of jobs before settling on what had become an incredibly successful career in music.

In 1972, Luther met Ken Harper, who included Vandross' song "Everbody Rejoice (A Brand New Day)" in the hit Broadway show *THE WIZ.* (The song was also featured in the Diana Ross / Michael Jackson movie of the same name.) Two years later, Luther received another important career break when David Bowie asked him to arrange and sing backgrounds on the *YOUNG AMERICANS* LP (including Luther's song "Fascination") as well as tour with the British star. Through Bowie, Luther met Bette Midler and later sang on both Bette's *SONGS FOR THE NEW DEPRESSION* and on the road with her. Midler's producer Arif Mardin was so impressed with Luther's intuitive musical sense that he called him for sessions with Carly Simon, Chaka Khan, and the Average White Band, among others.

On the strength of his session reputation, Vandross formed his own group, a progressive R&B vocal group called Luther. Signed to Atlantic / Cotillion Records, the act scored with "It's Good For The Soul" and "Funky Music Is A Part Of Me," and performed with many different artists including the late Marvin Gaye at New York's Radio City Music Hall in 1977. When the group eventually splintered, Luther embarked on a highly lucrative career as a jingle singer for corporate clients like 7-Up and Kentucky Fried Chicken. His work as lead vocalist for two studio groups, Change and Bionic Boogie (of "Hot Butterfly" fame), helped to bring Luther's immediately identifiable sound to national attention during the disco days of the late Seventies.

After continuous touring with (among others) Bette Midler, Todd Rundgren, and Roberta Flack; and session work for the likes of the J. Geils Band, Barbra Streisand, Donna Summer, Burt Bacharach and Quincy Jones, Luther Vandross signed with Epic Records as a solo artist in 1981. His recorded output since then speaks for itself. In _BILLBOARD_, the respected critic Nelson George called Luther "perhaps the preeminent singer in black music today," while _THE NEW YORK TIMES'_ Stephen Holden cited Luther as "the most promising all-around pop / soul craftsman (singer, songwriter, producer) to emerge in the Eighties."

The accolades have mounted through the second half of the decade. There were spellbinding television appearances on Patti Labelle's 1985 NBC special, on Luther's own BBC-TV concert special in 1987, and as host of the first annual "Soul Train Awards" in 1987. They only confirmed what record buyers have discovered with each new Vandross album: Quite simply, Luther is one of the finest male vocalists of his generation, one whose appeal transcends all musical and social boundaries.

In 1988 came _ANY LOVE_, produced by Luther Vandross with Marcus Miller and featuring songs penned by Luther and stalwart colleague Nat Adderly Jr. and new collaborators Hubert Eaves III and (from Scritti Politti) David Gamson. "I'd say I'm a more relaxed singer now," said Luther at the time of _ANY LOVE_'s release, "and when I listen to this record, I hear the old values I've always used in my work. Yet being my sixth album, there's a certain polish that comes with time, knowing more and more what works for me musically. I always go with what feels good, and if it feels right musically, I do it."

It's clear that the public feels good about what Luther Vandross does musically: _ANY LOVE_ brought him three more hit singles in "I Really Didn't Mean It," "For You To Love," and the title track. Luther refers to the latter as "one of the most personal pieces of material I've written. I wanted people to know that I have a life, that I go through the same personal challenges as everyone else. _ANY LOVE_ expresses that."

During the past year, Luther's been busier than ever. He guested on the very first segment of the highly successful Arsenio Hall show and on NBC's "Saturday Night Live." He was the subject of simultaneous cover stories in both _EBONY_ and _JET_; the accompanying photo spread took readers into Luther's exclusive Beverly Hills home, formerly owned by gossip columnist Rona Barrett.

With special liner notes from Aretha Franklin, Dionne Warwick and Arsenio Hall that underscore the respect and admiration he commands in the entertainment industry, _THE BEST OF LUTHER VANDROSS, THE BEST OF LOVE_ stands as a testament to one of the most prodigious musical talents of our time — on Epic Cassettes, Compact Discs and Records.

SEARCHING

By MARIO MALAVASI
and PAUL SLADE

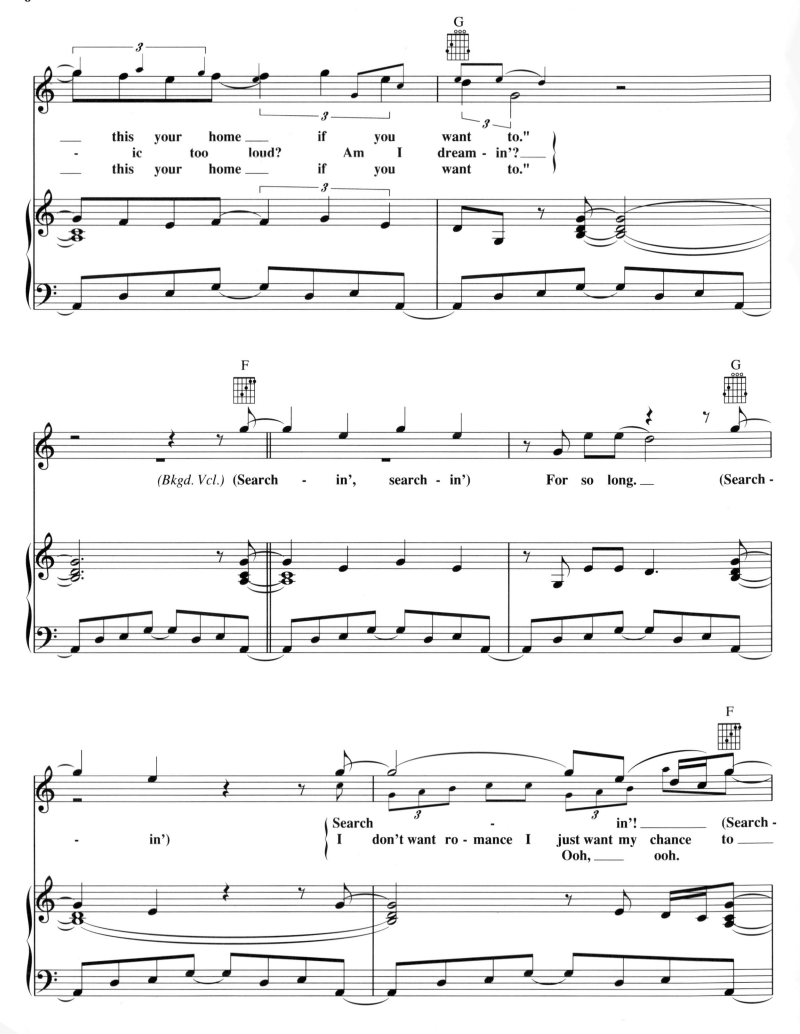

THE GLOW OF LOVE

By DAVID ROMANI,
W. GARFIELD and MARIO MALAVASI

NEVER TOO MUCH

Words and Music by
LUTHER VANDROSS

Moderate Funk

I can't fool my - self __ I don't want no - bod -
Woke up to - day, __ looked at your pic -

IF THIS WORLD WERE MINE

By MARVIN GAYE

SINCE I LOST MY BABY

By WILLIAM "SMOKEY" ROBINSON
and WARREN MOORE

PROMISE ME

Words and Music by
LUTHER VANDROSS

A HOUSE IS NOT A HOME

Lyric by HAL DAVID
Music by BURT BACHARACH

'TIL MY BABY COMES HOME

Words and Music by LUTHER VANDROSS
and MARCUS MILLER

There's a whole___ lot of girls___
I get weak___ in the knees___ my
Ev-'ry night___ when I sleep___ I

mess-in' a - round.___   try - in' to get___ me.
hands start a shak - in'   head gets to ach - in'.
dream of my ba - by,   she's such a la - dy.

IF ONLY FOR ONE NIGHT

By BRENDA RUSSELL

Let me hold you___ tight   if on - ly for one___

CREEPIN'

By STEVIE WONDER

And it's __ gon' be __ to-night. __

I _____ can ____ hear ____ you sigh-in'. Say _____ you'll ____ stay
On _____ the beach ____ we're sit-tin', hug-gin',__ squeez-

SUPERSTAR/
UNTIL YOU COME BACK TO ME

Key of "G"

SUPERSTAR
Words and Music by LEON RUSSELL
and BONNIE BRAMLETT

UNTIL YOU COME BACK TO ME
By STEVIE WONDER,
MORRIS BROADNAX and CLARENCE PAUL

SUPERSTAR

UNTIL YOU COME BACK TO ME

STOP TO LOVE

Words and Music by LUTHER VANDROSS
and NAT ADDERLEY, JR.

Late - ly love keeps keep-ing me 'wake
___ my love has al - ways been on ___

SO AMAZING

Words and Music by
LUTHER VANDROSS

Slowly with feeling

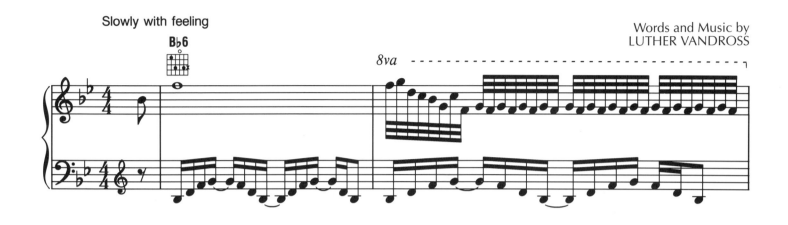

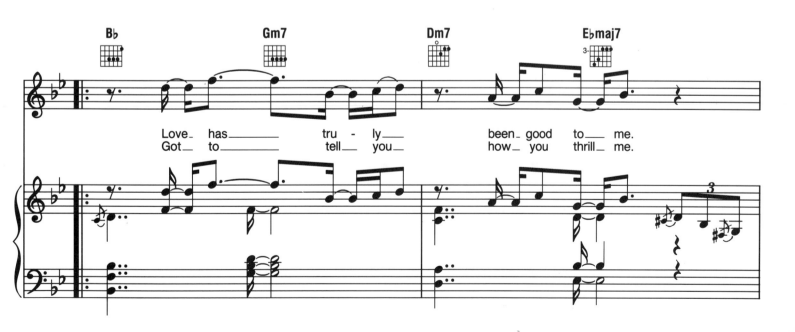

Love has___ tru-ly___ been_ good to__ me.
Got_ to___ tell_ you__ how_ you thrill__ me.

Not__ e - ven__ one sad__ day, or min - ute have__ I had__ since you've come__ my way.
I'm hap - py as__ I can__ be. You have come__ and it's changed__ my whole world,__

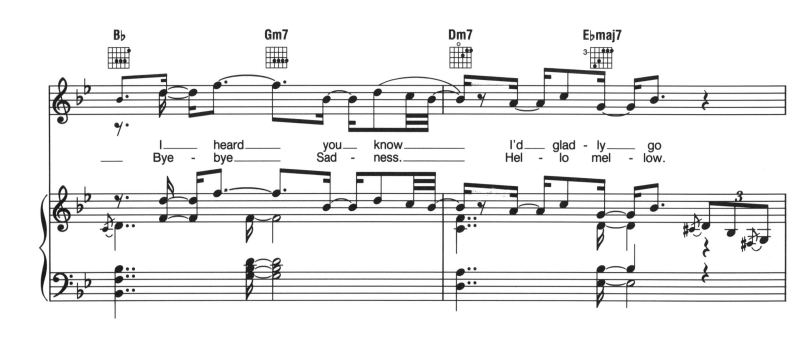

I__ heard_____ you know_____ I'd__ glad - ly__ go
Bye - bye_____ Sad - ness._____ Hel - lo mel - low.

an - y - where__you take__ me. It's so a - maz - ing to__ be loved.__ I'd
What a won - der - ful day. It's so a - maz - ing to__ be loved.__ I'd

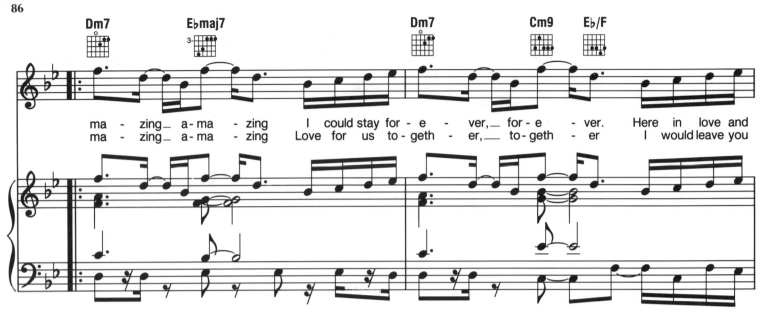

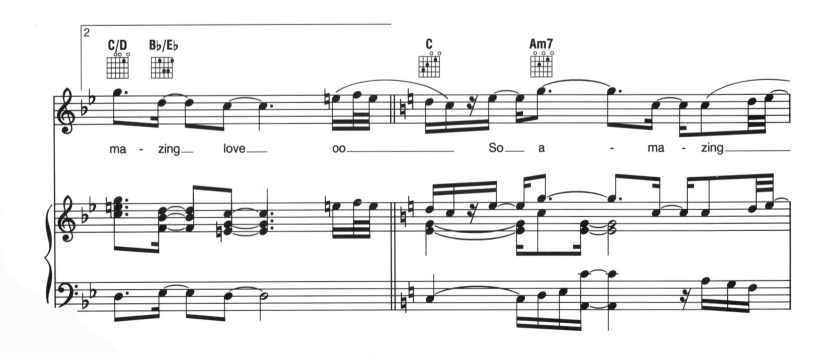

THERE'S NOTHING BETTER THAN LOVE

Words and Music by LUTHER VANDROSS
& JOHN "SKIP" ANDERSON

Slowly

I fell a-sleep late last night and I dreamed the night and al-most half the day a-way. I just got up so that I could hear her say,

GIVE ME THE REASON

Words and Music by LUTHER VANDROSS
and NAT ADDERLEY, JR.

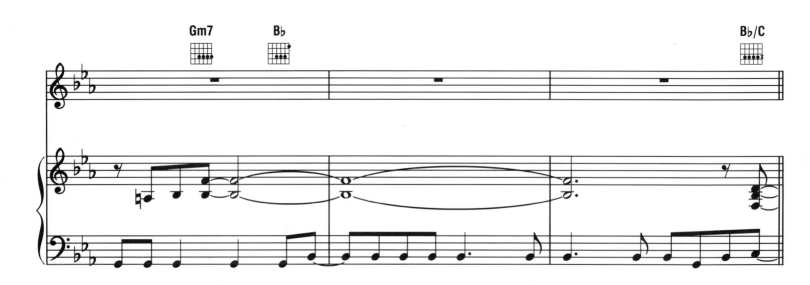

98

Verse 2:
I was secure and so glad
There was you to love.
What in the world would I
Ever do without us?
But, it's getting clear that
I have to get over you.

ANY LOVE

Words and Music by LUTHER VANDROSS
and MARCUS MILLER

I speak to my-self some-times _ and I say, "Oh _ my, in a lot of ways you're a luck-y guy. And oh, _____ now all you need is a chance to try an - y love." _

I REALLY DIDN'T MEAN IT

Words and Music by LUTHER VANDROSS
and MARCUS MILLER

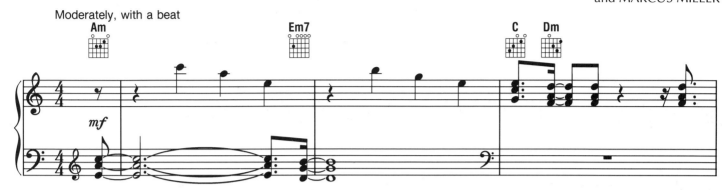

real - ly did - n't mean it._____ (mean it)_____ And her love is love, so

fine and so___ for real.___ I want the world to

know the way___ I feel._____ She's my girl and my

best friend_____ and I real - ly did - n't mean it._____ Hey,_____ yeah.___

TREAT YOU RIGHT

Words and Music by LUTHER VANDROSS
and MARCUS MILLER

MCA MUSIC PUBLISHING

HERE AND NOW

Words and Music by TERRY STEELE
and DAVID ELLIOT

F#m7(♭5)   B7(♭9)   Cmaj7   G/B

share   makes life___ so___ sweet._____ To-
more___ and more each day.___

C(add9)/E   Cm6/E♭   G/D   C(add9)

geth - er we'll al - ways   be.___
Noth - ing can take___ your___ love a - way.___

G(add9)/B B7/D#   Em7   G/B

This pledge of love___ feels   so   right,___ and___ ooh,_____ I___ need___
More than ah - just___   a   dream.___   I___ need___

Cmaj9   F#m7(♭5)   A/B

_____ you.___
_____ you.___   Yeah.}   Here   and   now,___